Asia

A Buddy Book
by

Cheryl Striveildi

ABDO
Publishing Company

VISIT US AT
www.abdopub.com

Published by Buddy Books, an imprint of ABDO Publishing Company, 4940 Viking Drive, Edina, Minnesota 55435. Copyright © 2003 by Abdo Consulting Group, Inc. International copyrights reserved in all countries. No part of this book may be reproduced in any form without written permission from the publisher.

Printed in the United States.

Edited by: Christy DeVillier
Contributing Editors: Matt Ray, Michael P. Goecke
Graphic Design: M. Hosley
Image Research: Deborah Coldiron
Photographs: Corbis, Corel, Minden Pictures,

Library of Congress Cataloging-in-Publication Data

Striveildi, Cheryl, 1971-
    Continents. Asia / Cheryl Striveildi.
        p. cm.
    Includes index.
    Summary: Provides a simple introduction to some of the geographical features of the continent of Asia.
    ISBN 1-57765-960-0
        1. Asia—Juvenile literature. [1. Asia.] I. Title: Asia. II. Title.

DS5 .S75 2003
950—dc21

                                                             2002074665

Table of Contents

Seven Continents

Water covers most of the earth. Land covers the rest. The earth has seven main land areas, or continents. The seven continents are:

 North America

 Africa

 South America

 Asia

 Europe

 Australia

 Antarctica

There is much to see in Asia

Asia is the world's largest continent. Asia's land covers about 17,213,300 square miles (44,579,000 sq km).

Asia is sometimes called the Old World. Indeed, Asia's history goes back more than 5,000 years. The first cities in the world began in Asia. Asians were the first to write and make paper. Today, Asia is a mix of old and new customs.

Where Is Asia?

The top half of the earth is the Northern Hemisphere. Asia is in the Northern Hemisphere.

East of Asia is the Pacific Ocean. South of Asia is the Indian Ocean. The Arctic Ocean lies north of Asia.

Europe is west of Asia. Africa is to the southwest. The northeast tip of Asia is close to North America. The Bering Strait lies between Asia and North America.

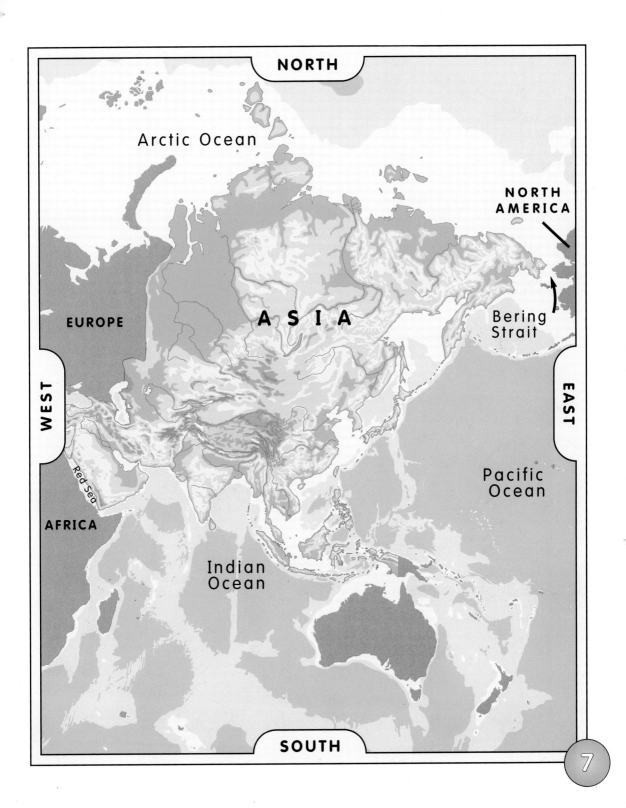

NORTH

Arctic Ocean

NORTH
AMERICA

EUROPE

ASIA

Bering
Strait

WEST

EAST

Red Sea

Pacific
Ocean

AFRICA

Indian
Ocean

SOUTH

Western Asia is joined to Europe.
Some people call the landmass of Asia
and Europe "Eurasia." But most people
believe they are two different continents.
This is because Asia is very different
from Europe.

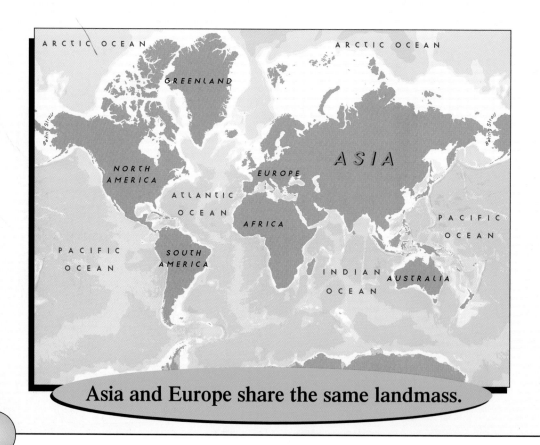

Asia and Europe share the same landmass.

Russia is the world's largest country. Russia lies partly in Europe. But most of Russia is in Asia. This part of Russia is called Siberia. It gets very cold in Siberia.

Siberia has long, cold winters.

China is the third-largest country in the world. It is in eastern Asia. The Chinese way of life goes back thousands of years.

Asia has more than 40 other countries. Some of them are on islands. Two tropical island countries are Indonesia and the Philippines.

Japan is another island country. It lies in the Pacific Ocean. Storms called typhoons hit Japan every year. These typhoons bring strong winds and rain.

Tokyo, Japan

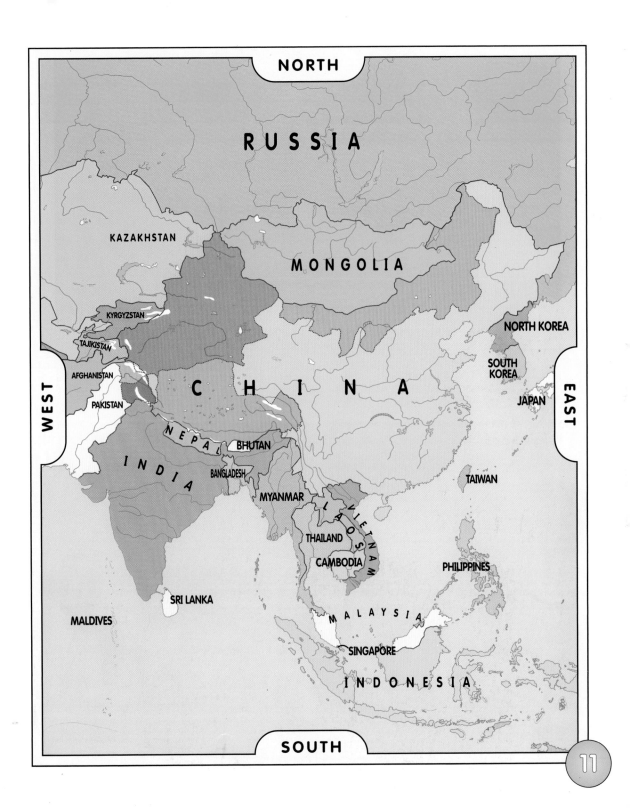

The Most People

Asia has more people than any other continent. More than three billion people live in Asia. This is more than half of the world's population. Population is the number of people living in one place.

Asia's cities are full of people.

Bikes help people get around in China's crowded cities.

More than one billion people live in China. China has the highest population in the world. India has the second-highest population.

China and India have hundreds of languages. India's national language is Hindi. China's national language is Mandarin Chinese. Chinese does not have an alphabet like English. Written Chinese does not look like English at all.

Chinese is one of the oldest languages in the world.

Religions And Temples

This Chinese temple was built in 1420.

Many religions began in Asia. Three of them are Hinduism, Buddhism, and Islam. Asia has many beautiful, old temples. Many Asian temples are hundreds of years old.

Tallest Mountains

The tallest mountains in the world are in Asia. The world's tallest mountain is Mount Everest. Mount Everest's **peak** is the highest point in the world. This mountain is in the Himalayas.

Mount Everest

Red Panda

The Himalaya Mountains are in southern Asia. They stretch from Pakistan to China. Bears, red pandas, and snow leopards live in the Himalayas. Red pandas look like raccoons. They eat bamboo leaves.

The Karakoram Mountains are north of the Himalayas. The Godwin Austen mountain is there. It is the second-highest mountain in the world.

It gets cold and windy high in Asia's mountains. Mount Everest has snow year round. No trees grow on the highest mountain peaks.

Peak of Mount Everest

The Sherpa

   The Sherpa people live in mountain villages of Nepal and India. They know a lot about the Himalaya Mountains. Mountain hikers often hire Sherpa guides. They can guide hikers up the steep mountains.

Lakes And Rivers

A lake is a body of water with land on all sides. The Caspian Sea is really a saltwater lake. It is the biggest lake in the world. The Caspian Sea lies between Asia and Europe.

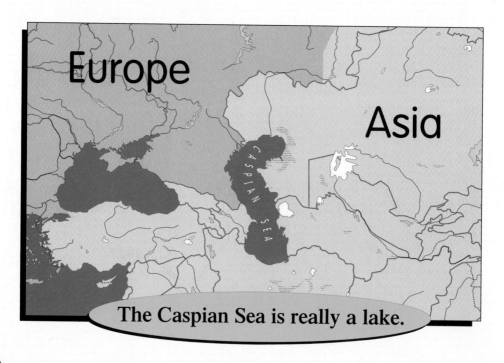

The Caspian Sea is really a lake.

The longest river in Asia is the Yangtze. It is in China. The Indus River is in Pakistan. The Ganges River is in India.

Asia's rivers are important for farming. They bring water to farmlands. One important Asian crop is rice. It grows well in tropical areas of southern Asia. China, Japan, and India have many rice farms.

Rice farms need a lot of water.

Wet fields of rice are called paddies.

Monsoons

Southern Asia has monsoons every year. Monsoons are strong winds. In the winter, monsoons bring dry, cold air. This is the dry season.

Monsoons bring rain during the wet season. The wet season lasts from spring to early fall.

Monsoons are important to India, Bangladesh, and Myanmar. Much of India's water comes from monsoons. Farmers need monsoon rains to water their crops. Sometimes, monsoons bring too much rain. Too much rain causes floods.

Gobi Desert

Western and central Asia have dry, desert areas. The Gobi Desert is in southern Mongolia. Wild gerbils, camels, and golden eagles live in the dry Gobi Desert.

Gobi Desert

Visiting Asia

The Taj Mahal is a famous building in India. It is the biggest tomb in the world. A tomb is a special building that houses the dead. The Taj Mahal was built for Mumtaz Mahal. She was a princess.

Taj Mahal

Army of Clay Soldiers

In 1974, Chinese farmers dug up some old clay soldier statues. These clay soldiers are thousands of years old. They were built to guard the tomb of the first Chinese emperor. This clay army has more than 7,400 soldiers.

People can see the army of clay soldiers in Shaanxi, China.

Another famous sight in Asia is the Great Wall of China. It was built hundreds of years ago. At one time, the Great Wall was 4,500 miles (7,242 km) long. People from around the world visit the Great Wall each year.

The Great Wall of China

A walkway on the Great Wall of China

Asia

🐾 Asia is the world's largest continent.

🐾 Asia has more people than any other continent.

🐾 Mount Everest is the tallest mountain in the world.

🐾 The Caspian Sea is the biggest lake in the world.

🐾 The Yangtze River is the third-longest river in the world.

🐾 The lowest point in Asia is the Dead Sea. It is the lowest point in the world.

🐾 The Taj Mahal is the biggest tomb in the world.

Important Words

continent one of the earth's seven main land areas.

customs the way of life common to a group of people. Language, food, clothes, and religion are some customs.

hemisphere one half of the earth.

monsoons strong winds in southern Asia.

peak mountaintop.

tomb a special building that houses the dead.

tropical weather that is warm and wet.

typhoon a tropical storm that brings heavy rain and wind.

Web Sites

Would you like to learn more about Asia?
Please visit ABDO Publishing Company on the World Wide Web to find web site links about Asia.
These links are routinely monitored and updated to provide the most current information available.

www.abdopub.com

Index